John Thompson's Modern Course for the Piano — SECOND GRADE

POPULAR PIANO SOLOS

Pop Hits, Broadway, Movies and More!

Book: ISBN 978-1-4234-0905-2
Book/CD: ISBN 978-1-4234-1253-3

WILLIS MUSIC

EXCLUSIVELY DISTRIBUTED BY

HAL•LEONARD®
CORPORATION
7777 W. BLUEMOUND RD. P.O. BOX 13819 MILWAUKEE, WI 53213

Visit Hal Leonard Online at
www.halleonard.com

Contents

The Addams Family Theme 34

Alley Cat 4

Do-Re-Mi 16

I Could Have Danced All Night 25

The Masterpiece 36

Memory 30

My Heart Will Go On (Love Theme from 'Titanic') 10

Nadia's Theme 13

Raiders March 22

Sway (Quién Será) 7

A Time for Us (Love Theme) 19

Alley Cat

Use with John Thompson's Modern Course for the Piano
SECOND GRADE BOOK, after page 6.

By Frank Bjorn
Arranged by Eric Baumgartner

6

Sway
(Quién Será)
Use after page 11.

English Words by Norman Gimbel
Spanish Words and Music by Pablo Beltrán Ruiz
Arranged by Eric Baumgartner

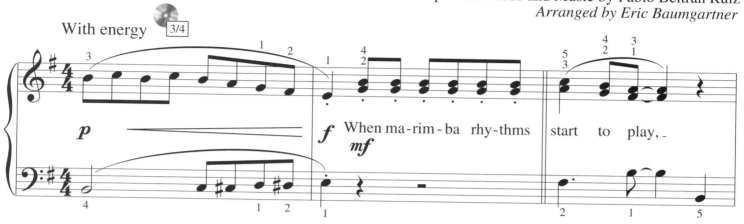

When ma-rim-ba rhy-thms start to play, dance with me, — make me sway. — Like the la-zy o-cean

hugs the shore, — hold me close, — sway me more. —

Like a flow-er bend-ing in the breeze, — bend with me, —

sway with ease. ___ When we dance you have a way with me, ___

stay with me, ___ sway with me. ___ Oth - er danc - ers may

be on the floor, dear, but my eyes will see on - ly you.

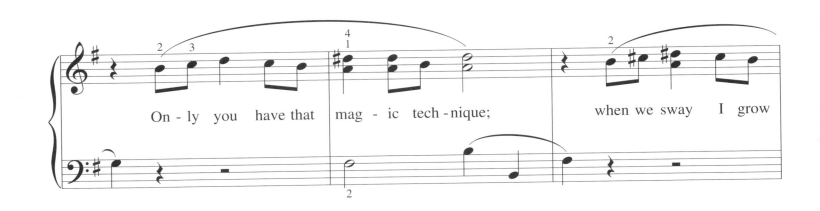

On - ly you have that mag - ic tech - nique; when we sway I grow

weak.   I can hear the sound of   vi - o - lins, —

mf

long   be - fore —   it   be - gins. —   Make me thrill as   on - ly

you   know how, —   sway   me smooth, —   sway   me now. —

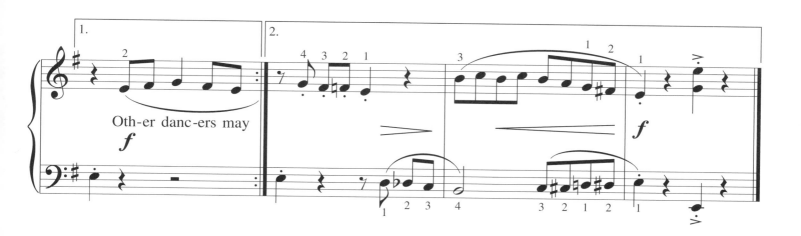

Oth-er danc-ers may   *f*

My Heart Will Go On

(Love Theme from 'Titanic')

from the Paramount and Twentieth Century Fox Motion Picture TITANIC

Use after page 16.

Music by James Horner
Lyric by Will Jennings
Arranged by Eric Baumgartner

Nadia's Theme

from THE YOUNG AND THE RESTLESS

Use after page 21.

By Barry DeVorzon and Perry Botkin, Jr.
Arranged by Eric Baumgartner

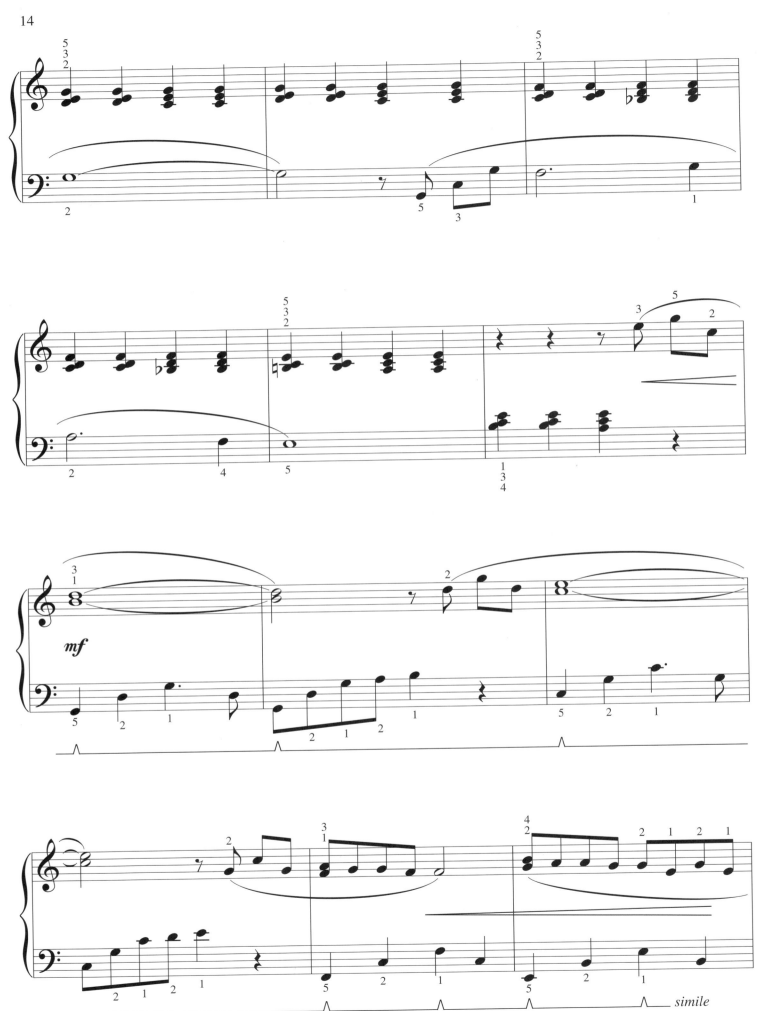

Do-Re-Mi

from THE SOUND OF MUSIC

Use after page 28.

Lyrics by Oscar Hammerstein II
Music by Richard Rodgers
Arranged by Eric Baumgartner

Doe, a deer, a fe - male deer, Ray, a drop of gold - en sun, Me, a name I call my - self, Far, a long, long way to run. Sew, a nee-dle pull-ing

thread, La, a note to fol-low sew,

Tea, a drink with jam and bread That will bring us back to

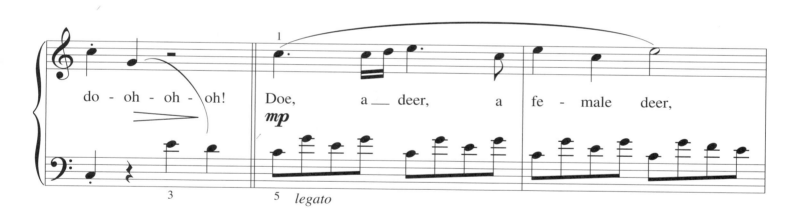

do - oh - oh - oh! Doe, a __ deer, a fe - male deer,

legato

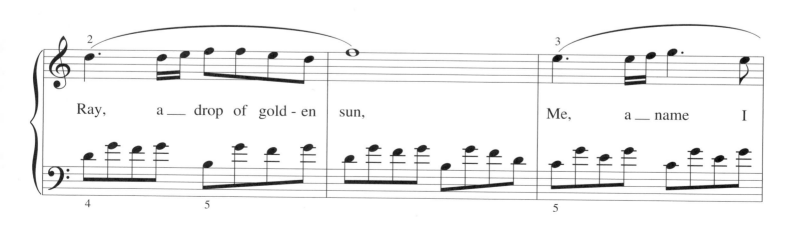

Ray, a __ drop of gold - en sun, Me, a __ name I

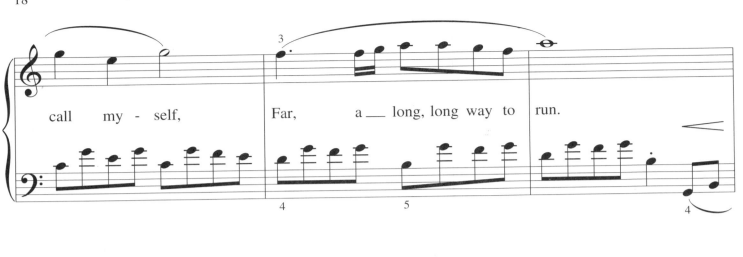

call my - self, Far, a __ long, long way to run.

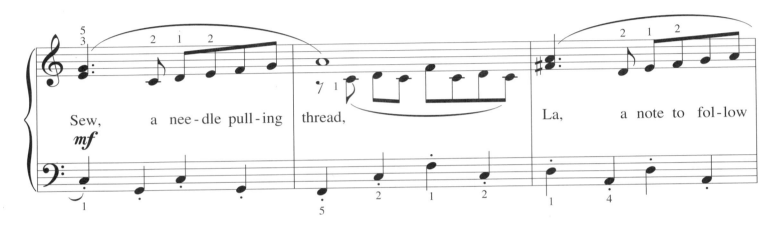

Sew, a nee - dle pull - ing thread, La, a note to fol - low

mf

sew, Tea, a drink with jam and bread That will

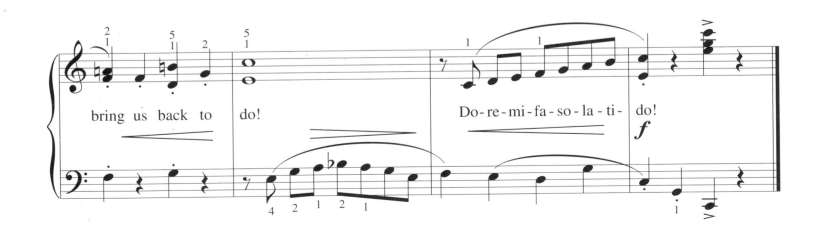

bring us back to do! Do - re - mi - fa - so - la - ti - do!

f

A Time for Us
(Love Theme)
from the Paramount Picture ROMEO AND JULIET
Use after page 35.

Words by Larry Kusik and Eddie Snyder
Music by Nino Rota
Arranged by Eric Baumgartner

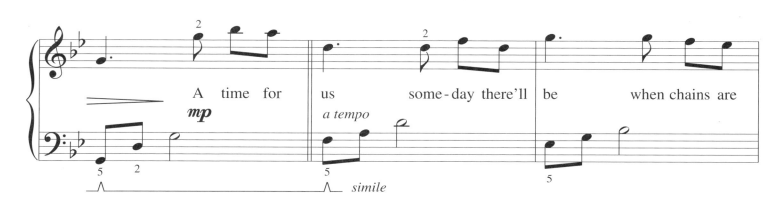

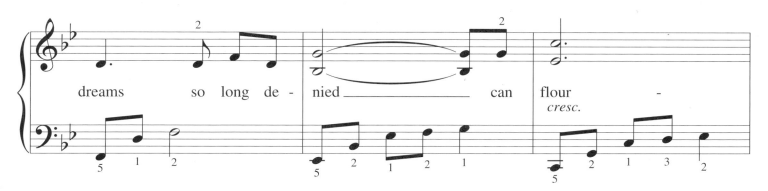

20

sure - ly through ev - 'ry storm. A time for us some - day there'll

be _____ a new world, _____ a

world of shin - ing hope for you and me.

mf　　　*rit.*　　　*mp* *a tempo*

rit.　　　*pp*

Raiders March

from the Paramount Motion Picture RAIDERS OF THE LOST ARK

Use after page 45.

Music by John Williams
Arranged by Eric Baumgartner

I Could Have Danced All Night

from MY FAIR LADY

Use after page 56.

Words by Alan Jay Lerner
Music by Frederick Loewe
Arranged by Eric Baumgartner

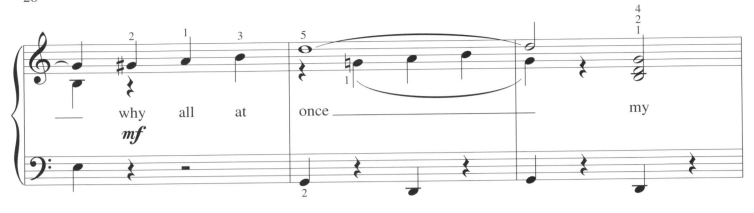

why all at once _____ my

mf

heart took flight. _____

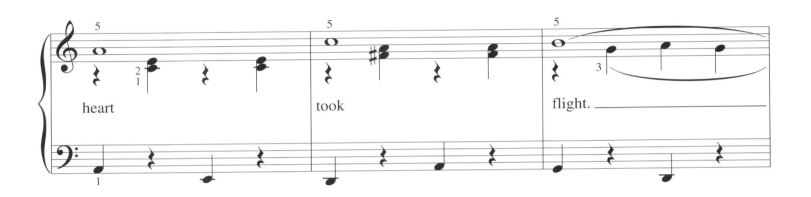

f I on - ly

know _____ when he _____

mf

Memory

from CATS

Use after page 64.

Music by Andrew Lloyd Webber
Text by Trevor Nunn after T.S. Eliot
Arranged by Eric Baumgartner

beat _____ a fa - tal - is - tic

warn - ing. _____ Some - one

mut - ters ___ and a street lamp gut - ters ___ and

soon it will be morn - ing. _____
dim.

Day - light. _____ I must wait for the sun - rise, _____
mp

The Addams Family Theme
Theme from the TV Show and Movie
Use after page 70.

Music and Lyrics by Vic Mizzy
Arranged by Eric Baumgartner

creep-y and they're kook-y, mys- te - ri - ous and spook-y, they're al - to-geth-er ook-y, the

The Masterpiece
the TV Theme from MASTERPIECE THEATRE
Use after page 76.

By J.J. Mouret and Paul Parnes
Arranged by Eric Baumgartner

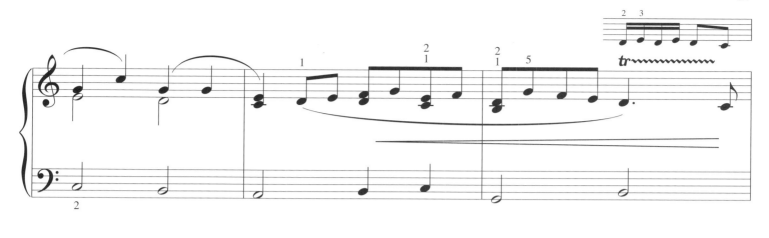

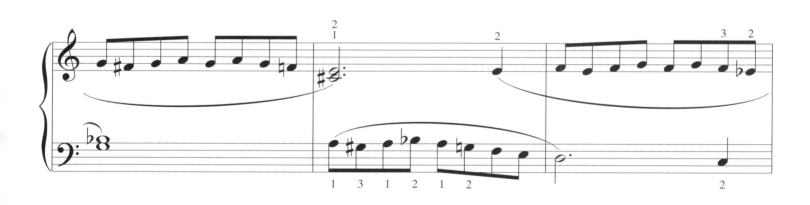

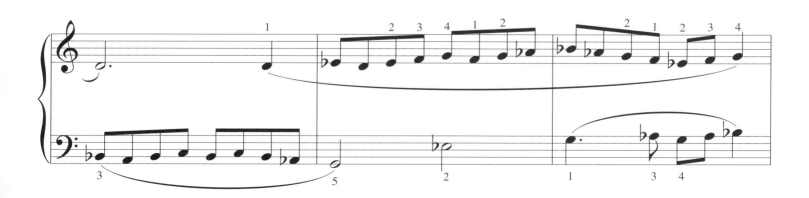

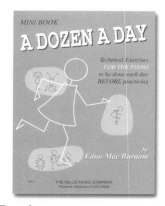

A Dozen a Day
Piano Series

by Edna Mae Burnam

Each book contains short warm-up
exercises to be played at the beginning of
the student's practice session. Performing
these technical exercises will help develop
strong hands and flexible fingers.

Mini Book

00404073	Book only	$3.95
00406472	Book/CD	$8.95
00406474	CD only	$9.95
00406475	GM Disk only	$9.95

Preparatory Book

00414222	Book only	$3.95
00406476	Book/CD	$8.95
00406479	CD only	$9.95
00406477	Book/GM Disk	$13.95
00406480	GM Disk only	$9.95

Book 1

00413366	Book only	$3.95
00406481	Book/CD	$8.95
00406483	CD only	$9.95
00406482	Book/GM Disk	$13.90
00406484	GM Disk only	$9.95

Book 2

00413826	Book only	$3.95
00406485	Book/CD	$8.95
00406487	CD only	$9.95
00406486	Book/GM Disk	$13.90
00406488	GM Disk only	$9.95

Book 3

00414136	Book only	$4.95
00416760	Book/CD	$9.95

Book 4

00415686	Book only	$5.95
00416761	Book/CD	$10.95

Play with Ease
in Many Keys

00416395	Book only	$3.95

Sportacular
Warmups Series

by Carolyn Miller
Progressive finger "workouts"
using sports themes and characters
elementary-level piano students will love!

00406292	Book 1	$6.95
00406293	Book 2	$6.95
00406294	Book 3	$6.95
00406295	Book 4	$6.95

TECHNIC –
ALL THE WAY!

by William Gillock

While there are many books on piano
technique available today, few, if any,
provide a sequence of exercises for
the small, untrained hand of the young
beginner and an explanation as to how
to achieve the desired results. This series
offers guidance to the teacher and student
regarding basic principles of technical ease.

00404213	Level 1A	EE	$2.25
00404214	Level 1B	EE	$2.25
00404460	Level 2A	ME	$2.50
00404895	Level 2B	LE	$2.95

Spectacular Piano Solos

from

WILLIS MUSIC

www.willispianomusic.com

Early Elementary

00416702	Big Green Frog/Carolyn C. Setliff	$2.95
00406670	Cookies/Carolyn Miller	$2.95
00404218	Fog at Sea/William Gillock	$2.95
00416763	I Can!/Carolyn C. Setliff	$2.95
00406628	The Itsy Bitsy Elephant/Cheryl Finn and Eamonn Morris	$1.95
00406537	Let's Dance!/Robert Donahue	$1.95
00412099	Moccasin Dance/John Thompson	$1.95
00416783	My Missing Teeth/Carolyn C. Setliff	$2.95
00416685	Pets/Al Rita	$2.95

Mid-Elementary

00416780	The Acrobat/Carolyn Miller	$2.95
00406806	Chit Chat/Robert Donahue	$1.95
00406593	Clown Act/Matthew Ordaz	$2.95
00416803	The Dancing Bears/Carolyn Miller	$2.95
00416746	Forest Murmurs/Carolyn C. Setliff	$2.95
00406436	A New Day/Carolyn C. Setliff	$2.95
00406390	Night of Fright/Randall Hartsell	$1.95
00416728	Seahorse Serenade/Carolyn C. Setliff	$2.95
00416674	Seaside Dancer/Ronald Bennett	$2.50
00416785	Watermelon Sunset/Randall Hartsell	$2.95
00416730	Wildflower Waltz/Robert Donahue	$2.95

Later Elementary

00416840	At The Ballet/Carolyn C. Setliff	$2.99
00406667	Classic Sonatina in C/Carolyn C. Setliff	$3.95
00408976	Drifting Clouds/Lois Rehder Holmes	$2.50
00416786	Egyptian Journey/Randall Hartsell	$2.95
00406367	Ghostly Steps/Ernest Kramer	$1.95
00406357	Goldfish Gavotte/Melody Bober	$1.95
00416747	Halloween Hop/Al Rita	$2.95
00416553	Hummingbird/Robert Donahue	$2.95
00405553	Jaguar Strut/Ronald Bennett	$1.95
00406744	Just Jesting!/Ronald Bennett	$1.95
00406536	Ladybug Waltz/Robert Donahue	$1.95
00405918	Monkey on a Stick/Lynn Freeman Olson	$2.95
00406356	Mountain Dance/Melody Bober	$1.95
00406364	Mysterious Castle/Matthew Ordaz	$2.95
00406552	Parisian Waltz/Robert Donahue	$2.95
00416565	Punch and Judy (Puppet Dance)/Eric Baumgartner	$2.95
00416781	The Race Car/Carolyn Miller	$2.95
00416664	Roses in Twilight/Carolyn C. Setliff	$2.95
00406767	Rushing Brook/Carolyn C. Setliff	$1.95
00416489	Russian Ballet/Deborah Ellis Suarez	$1.95
00406883	Sassy/Rosemary Hughey	$1.95
00416531	Shingle Shaker Rag/Glenda Austin	$1.95
00406564	Showdown/Ronald Bennett	$2.95
00406681	Spanish Delight/David Karp	$1.95
00416820	Star Wonders/Randall Hartsell	$2.99
00416779	Sunrise at San Miguel/Ronald Bennett	$2.95
00406359	Thingama-Gigue/Melody Bober	$1.95
00406798	Tiffany Twilight/Claudette Hudelson	$1.95
00406882	Under the Stars/Rosemary Hughey	$1.95

Early Intermediate

00406378	Alabama Boogie/Alexander Peskanov	$1.95
00416534	Alexandra's Dream/Carolyn Miller	$1.95
00406810	Apache Drums/Carolyn C. Setliff	$2.95
00406880	Awesome!/Ronald Bennett	$2.50
00406459	Ballad in A Minor/Edmon Perkins	$1.95
00406242	Balletto/Alexander Peskanov	$1.95
00406408	Bangkok Market/Edward Grossman	$1.95
00406511	Calm Sea/David Karp	$1.95
00416834	Canopy of Stars/Randall Hartsell	$2.99
00416647	Carnival March/Carolyn C. Setliff	$2.95
00406399	Clouds at Sunset/Robert Kelley	$1.95

00416686	Cuckoo Clock/Deborah Ellis Suarez	$2.95
00406815	Dance Caprice/George Kiorpes	$1.95
00406887	Dancing Waters/Deborah Ellis Suarez	$2.95
00416543	Dragon Mist/Lois Rehder Holmes	$2.95
00416548	Enchanted Tale/Matthew Ordaz	$1.95
00406335	Farewell Waltz/Alexander Peskanov	$1.95
00415585	Flamenco/William Gillock	$2.95
00416717	Foot-Stampin' Rag/Robert Kelley	$2.95
00406447	A Ghostly Tarantella/George Kiorpes	$1.95
00406367	Ghostly Steps/Ernest Kramer	$1.95
00406194	Hungarian Dance/Melody Bober	$1.95
00416676	International Spies/Deborah Ellis Suarez	$2.95
00416703	The Joplin Jubilee Rag/Glenda Austin	$2.95
00416568	Knick Knack/Eric Baumgartner	$1.95
00416699	Mango Tango/Robert Kelley	$2.95
00406448	Marche Macabre/George Kiorpes	$1.95
00416733	The Matador/Carolyn Miller	$2.95
00416687	Moonlit Night/Deborah Ellis Suarez	$2.95
00406800	My Beautiful Rose Garden/Claudette Hudelson	$1.95
00406422	Nocturne in A Minor/David Karp	$2.95
00406241	Reverie/George Kiorpes	$1.95
00406886	Rippling Waters/Rosemary Hughey	$1.95
00416665	Scamper/Robert Donahue	$2.50
00416829	Scherzo Nuovo/Eric Baumgartner	$2.99
00406595	Slavic Dance/Elaine Lebar	$1.95
00416842	Tarantella In G Minor/Glenda Austin	$2.99
00416782	Toccata Caprice/Carolyn C. Setliff	$2.95
00416675	Video Game Fever/Deborah Ellis Suarez	$2.95
00416681	Vista/Ronald Bennett	$2.50
00416663	Woodland Idyll/Frank Levin	$2.50

Mid-Intermediate

00416698	Black Key Blues/Alexander Peskanov	$2.95
00416821	Foggy Blues/Naoko Ikeda	$2.99
00416800	The Glacial Mermaid/Naoko Ikeda	$2.95
00416765	Grand Sonatina in G/Glenda Austin	$2.95
00406358	Home on the Range/Melody Bober	$1.95
00416700	Intermezzo in B Minor/arr. Frank Levin	$2.95
00406630	Jazz Suite No. 2/Glenda Austin	$3.95
00406701	Myths & Magic/Eric Baumgartner	$2.95
00416718	Patsy's Icicles/Deborah Ellis Suarez	$2.95
00416660	Poème/Carolyn C. Setliff	$2.95
00414627	Portrait of Paris/William Gillock	$1.95
00416844	Sea Tempest/Randall Hartsell	$2.99
00416719	Silhouette/Eugene Englert	$2.95
00406101	Smoky Mountain Rag/Alexander Peskanov	$1.95
00416701	Spanish Romance/arr. Frank Levin	$2.95
00416720	The Still Point/Scott Michal	$2.95
00416100	Three Jazz Preludes/William Gillock	$3.95
00416726	Tumbling Toccatina/Claudette Hudelson	$2.95
00416801	Two Romances/Naoko Ikeda	$3.95
00406025	Wind Chimes/Alexander Peskanov	$1.95

Later Intermediate

00416715	Hear the Spirit of America/Marilyn Briant and Andrew Zatman	$2.95
00416764	Romantic Rhapsody/Glenda Austin	$2.95
00409464	Tarantella/A. Pieczonka	$2.95

Early Advanced

00415166	Sleighbells in the Snow/William Gillock	$2.95
00405264	Valse Brillante/Glenda Austin	$2.95

FOR MORE INFORMATION, SEE YOUR LOCAL MUSIC DEALER,
OR WRITE TO:

HAL•LEONARD CORPORATION

7777 W. BLUEMOUND RD. P.O. BOX 13819 MILWAUKEE, WI 53213